WOULD YOU RATHER

FOOTBALL
EDITION

Some rules of the game.

Hi!

You have two choices.

You can play along with the questions alone.

You can also play with your friends, brothers, sisters, cousins, parents...

A referee organizes the game and asks the questions.

The players answer and explain their choice.
The one who is the funniest, most sincere or most intelligent, depending on the type of question, scores a point. The referee counts the points on a separate sheet.
Each question is different, it is up to the referee to honestly decide which answer is best.
Okay, have fun and enjoy the game.
Is everyone ready?
Let's go!

WOULD YOU RATHER

score a long-range 30-yard
shot into the top corner

OR

a sublime overhead kick

1

WOULD YOU RATHER

play in the Bundesliga (Germany)

OR

La Liga (Spain)

hello

WOULD YOU RATHER

defend against Erling Haaland

OR

defend against Kylian Mbappé

WOULD YOU RATHER

play for the Brazilian national team

OR

the Argentine national team

WOULD YOU RATHER

sign with your rival club and triple your salary

OR

stay at your club without earning more

WOULD YOU RATHER

have neon green hair for a week

OR

play in a ski suit for an entire practice

6

WOULD YOU RATHER

play with Mohamed Salah

OR

with Sadio Mané

WOULD YOU RATHER

have a practice at **3:00** am
that lasts one hour

OR

a practice at **3:00** pm
that lasts three hours

WOULD YOU RATHER

play for Inter Milan

OR

for AC Milan

9

WOULD YOU RATHER

miss a Panenka

OR

fall on the ground while trying a step-over

10

WOULD YOU RATHER

be coached by Jurgen Klopp

OR

Pep Guardiola

WOULD YOU RATHER

win the **League** while being a substitute all the season

OR

finish in the middle of the table while being a starter

WOULD YOU RATHER

play with Jadon Sancho

OR

Marcus Rashford

13

WOULD YOU RATHER

lob the keeper from
the midfield

OR

score a hattrick of ugly
goals

WOULD YOU RATHER

watch **Barcelona** vs. **Real Madrid**

OR

Liverpool vs. **Everton**

WOULD YOU RATHER

be the fastest player in your team

OR

the one with the most physical endurance

WOULD YOU RATHER

play for the Irish national team

OR

the Scottish one

17

WOULD YOU RATHER

be a ball boy for a match
Burnley vs. Crystal Palace

OR

for a quarter final at
Wimbledon

WOULD YOU RATHER

be called **Danny Drinkwater**

OR

David Seaman

WOULD YOU RATHER

sing and jump with the fans

OR

be in a quiet stand

20

WOULD YOU RATHER

play for **Bayern Munich**

OR

for **Borussia Dortmund**

WOULD YOU RATHER

be coached by Gareth Southgate

OR

by Arsène Wenger

WOULD YOU RATHER

win thanks to a refereeing error

OR

end the match with a draw

23

WOULD YOU RATHER

fart super loud every time you score a goal

OR

meow just a little every time your team concedes a goal

24

WOULD YOU RATHER

play with Lionel Messi

OR

Cristiano Ronaldo

25

WOULD YOU
RATHER

be a goalkeeper and have four arms

OR

be 8 feet tall

WOULD YOU RATHER

play in Major League Soccer (USA)

OR

in Ligue I (France)

WOULD YOU RATHER

get tackled by Sergio Ramos

OR

Ngolo Kanté

WOULD YOU RATHER

dribble past five players, shoot but hit the post

OR

score a really really super easy goal

WOULD YOU RATHER

have a soft drink after the
Saturday afternoon game

OR

an orange juice

30

WOULD YOU RATHER

play in the Russian Premier League and never see your family

OR

play as an amateur in your country and be able to see your relatives

WOULD YOU RATHER

leave the game because you have diarrhea

OR

because of a sprained ankle

WOULD YOU RATHER

play for Arsenal

OR

Tottenham

33

WOULD YOU
RATHER

celebrate a goal by rolling on the ground but landing on a dog turd

OR

clear the ball and it unfortunately hit your coach in the head

WOULD YOU RATHER

have a calm coach

OR

one that gets easily angry

35

WOULD YOU RATHER

play with Kevin de Bruyne

OR

Mason Mount

WOULD YOU RATHER

play for Manchester United

OR

Manchester City

37

WOULD YOU RATHER

play the Football Manager video game

OR

FIFA

38

WOULD YOU RATHER

win the **World Cup** but have to eat cauliflower at every meal for a year

OR

do not win it and eat whatever you want

WOULD YOU RATHER

be a coach

a chairman

40

WOULD YOU RATHER

play a game blindfolded

OR

with a kitten in each hand

WOULD YOU RATHER

play for Galatasaray

OR

Fenerbahçe

42

WOULD YOU RATHER

be the third best scorer in your league

OR

the best passer

WOULD YOU RATHER

play a match with Eric Cantona

OR

Zinédine Zidane

44

WOULD YOU RATHER

have Messi

OR

Mbappé on Fifa Ultimate Team

45

WOULD YOU RATHER

be physically strong

OR

be a great technical player

46

WOULD YOU RATHER

get an unfair red card

OR

your best buddy get hurt

47

WOULD YOU RATHER

win against Chelsea

OR

win against Leeds

48

WOULD YOU RATHER

get yelled at by your coach

OR

get yelled at by your dad when you make a lousy pass

WOULD YOU RATHER

play for the **Australian National Team**

OR

the **Canadian National Team**

50

WOULD YOU RATHER

completely miss a penalty kick to the point that you shoot the ball at the referee

OR

score an own-goal by kicking the ball with your butt

WOULD YOU RATHER

have Cavani's haircut

OR

Pep Guardiola's haircut

WOULD YOU RATHER

do the career of **Steven Gerrard**

OR

the career of **Paul Scholes**

WOULD YOU RATHER

hurt yourself playing foosball

OR

kicking a small water bottle

WOULD YOU RATHER

play for Paris Saint-Germain

OR

Olympique de Marseille

WOULD YOU RATHER

watch a match on Sky Sports

OR

BT Sports

WOULD YOU RATHER

hear **God Save The Queen**

OR

the **Champions League's** anthem

WOULD YOU RATHER

play with Pelé

OR

with Maradona

58

WOULD YOU RATHER

play with candy-made

OR

lead-made cleats

WOULD YOU RATHER

play with Paul Pogba

OR

with Fabinho

WOULD YOU RATHER

watch the Champions League Final on the sly and get an "E" on the math test the next day

OR

don't watch the Final but get an "A" on the test

WOULD YOU RATHER

be a referee for a match between **Liverpool and Arsenal**

OR

a spectator in the front row of the stands

WOULD YOU RATHER

watch Match of the Day

OR

Football Focus

WOULD YOU RATHER

play on grass

OR

synthetic field

64

WOULD YOU RATHER

simulate a foul and the opponent gets a red card

OR

do not simulate a foul and the opponent does not get a card

WOULD YOU RATHER

play against a super physical team

OR

against a super technical team

WOULD YOU RATHER

be the best player in the
Scottish Premiership

OR

an average player in the
English Premier League

WOULD YOU RATHER

play a match with a bowling ball

OR

a pound coin instead of a ball

WOULD YOU RATHER

do 150 push-ups

OR

run 10 laps of the field

69

WOULD YOU RATHER

be substituted five minutes
after the game started

OR

enter as a subsitute and the
referee blows the whistle to end
the match twenty seconds later

WOULD YOU RATHER

play when it is very hot

OR

when it is very cold

WOULD YOU RATHER

play with Haaland

OR

with Lewandowski as a center forward

WOULD YOU RATHER

play a match while it's raining beans

OR

while spectators all fall asleep

WOULD YOU RATHER

wear an **Adidas**

OR

a **Nike** jersey

WOULD YOU
RATHER

have to sniff the whole team's
socks at the end of the game

OR

wash all your teammates'
shoes

WOULD YOU RATHER

be interviewed in Kick

OR

FourFourTwo

76

WOULD YOU RATHER

substitute the injured goalkeeper although it is not your position

OR

substitute the striker although it is not your position either

WOULD YOU RATHER

be able to jump three yards high

OR

make ten yards tackles

WOULD YOU RATHER

draw **0-0** five times in a row and take **5 points**

OR

win **2** games **1-0** then lose **3** games **15-0** but take **6** points

WOULD YOU RATHER

be tall and very thin

OR

short and very strong

WOULD YOU RATHER

giggle while your coach is
motivating the team

OR

have a tomato thrown at
you by an opposing fan
during a game

81

WOULD YOU RATHER

play futsal

OR

beach soccer

82

WOULD YOU RATHER

play with Heung-min Son

OR

with Phil Foden

83

WOULD YOU RATHER

win the **FA Cup with your** hometown club

OR

win the **Champions League** with the club you hate the most

84

WOULD YOU RATHER

make a foul throw

OR

your opponent dribbles you pushing the ball between your legs

85

WOULD YOU RATHER

play FIFA

OR

play PEs

WOULD YOU RATHER

tell jokes with Wayne Rooney

OR

David Beckham

87

WOULD YOU RATHER

have your hair grow three feet every time you miss a shot

OR

throw a pound coin in the toilet every time you miss a pass

WOULD YOU RATHER

play in heavy fog

OR

snow

89

WOULD YOU RATHER

celebrate a goal you scored by
doing a **DAB**

OR

a back flip

90

WOULD YOU RATHER

sweat really a lot and stinking up the place

OR

not being able to walk for two days

WOULD YOU RATHER

play with **Harry Maguire** in central defense

OR

with **Virgil van Dijk**

WOULD YOU RATHER

be the best player in the world and have no buddies

OR

be an amateur player with ten true buddies

93

WOULD YOU RATHER

take the ball in the belly

OR

on the nose

WOULD YOU RATHER

play street football

OR

football on grass

95

WOULD YOU RATHER

play the Olympics

OR

play the Euro

WOULD YOU RATHER

play a game on **FUT** until the end although you lose **6-0** at halftime

OR

rage quit and go to the next game

97

WOULD YOU RATHER

suddenly fall asleep in the middle of a match

OR

being vomited on by an opponent

WOULD YOU RATHER

dribble your opponent by doing a sombrero

OR

a scorpion lift

WOULD YOU RATHER

be a centre-back

OR

a wing-back defender

100

WOULD YOU RATHER

play a game that lasts twelve
hours without any halftime

OR

have a math test that
lasts four hours

101

WOULD YOU RATHER

win the **Europa League** with the club you love

OR

the **Champions League** with **V**alladolid

WOULD YOU RATHER

score an own goal in the Champions League Final

OR

lose 10 league games in a row

103

WOULD YOU RATHER

play for Glasgow Rangers

OR

for Celtic Glasgow

WOULD YOU RATHER

have **100** million followers on Instagram

OR

1 million dollars

105

WOULD YOU RATHER

play on Playstation

OR

Xbox

WOULD YOU RATHER

play with baby diapers

OR

with a Teletubbies mask on your head

107

WOULD YOU RATHER

as a goalkeeper, help your team to win by saving a penalty in the last minute

OR

by scoring a goal, coming up for a corner

WOULD YOU RATHER

be coached by Marcelo Bielsa

OR

by Thomas Tuchel

WOULD YOU RATHER

play on a completely sloping field

OR

play on a field where there are fifteen camels wandering around

WOULD YOU RATHER

have bubbles coming out of your ears when you lose the ball

OR

ketchup coming out of your nose

WOULD YOU RATHER

face **David De Gea**

OR

Alisson on a one–on–one

WOULD YOU RATHER

play a game hopping

OR

crawling on the floor

WOULD YOU RATHER

become a late professional
player at 25

OR

retire young at 32

WOULD YOU RATHER

get Harry Kane's autograph

OR

Raheem Sterling's autograph

WOULD YOU RATHER

have the national record for the most career goals

OR

the record for the most club trophies won

WOULD YOU RATHER

play with ants in your shoes

OR

see your teammates cry during the whole game for no reason

WOULD YOU RATHER

win the **Ballon d'or** but lose the
World Cup

OR

win the **World Cup** without
winning the **Ballon d'or**

WOULD YOU RATHER

play for the French national team

the German national team

WOULD YOU RATHER

arrive at the stadium sitting on a donkey

OR

play the game wearing a tutu

120

Printed in Great Britain
by Amazon

73297319R00071